YOUR KNOWLEDGE HAS VALUE

- We will publish your bachelor's and master's thesis, essays and papers

- Your own eBook and book - sold worldwide in all relevant shops

- Earn money with each sale

Upload your text at www.GRIN.com
and publish for free

Bibliographic information published by the German National Library:

The German National Library lists this publication in the National Bibliography; detailed bibliographic data are available on the Internet at http://dnb.dnb.de .

Imprint:

Copyright © 2015 GRIN Verlag, Open Publishing GmbH
Print and binding: Books on Demand GmbH, Norderstedt Germany
ISBN: 9783668385856

This book at GRIN:

http://www.grin.com/en/e-book/352049/getting-it-right-for-every-child-expert-views-on-multi-agency-social

Hanin Rasheed

'Getting it Right for Every Child'. Expert views on multi agency social work and child welfare in Scotland

GRIN Publishing

GRIN - Your knowledge has value

Since its foundation in 1998, GRIN has specialized in publishing academic texts by students, college teachers and other academics as e-book and printed book. The website www.grin.com is an ideal platform for presenting term papers, final papers, scientific essays, dissertations and specialist books.

Visit us on the internet:

http://www.grin.com/

http://www.facebook.com/grincom

http://www.twitter.com/grin_com

Abstract

The research focused on investigating the potential impact of GRIFEC supporting the multi-agency working along with the service delivery of children care and assessment process. Qualitative study was conducted by the researcher by asking volunteers and social workers that have been working in the children care agency. Semi-structured interviews were conducted to identify the research questions which were developed. The research revealed that there had been a positive and potential impact of GRIFEC for supporting multi-agency working to assist children care. The strengths of the multi-agency working included a better collaboration, mutual working, awareness of the project, better care for children, and a better solution for a problem when a combination of different social workers and volunteers are present to care for the children. However, at the same time the volunteers and the social workers also believe that there are certain limitations which also need lights to be shed.

Contents

Chapter 1: Introduction

1.1 Research Background

As GIRFEC is a tested and maintained national approach for striving to work for the betterment of the children and young people living across Scotland, the researcher will carry out a research based study to look for the strengths and weakness since it was implemented (Scottish Government, 2015). The research by looking at the evaluation process, methods, techniques and frameworks which are carried out to identify and guard the children and their families and also how multiple agencies working in the same environment are influenced. In an association of the multi-agency working between parents and agencies is not a new expansion and for many years' importance has been placed on the involvement of inter-agency working. Though there are some advantageous results for professionals, patients and clients across some services (Leathard, 2003) there are number of cases and public inquiry reports that are reviewed which focuses on the child deaths across the UK and concludes that it has failed to be consistent and lacks teamwork between the agencies (Hammond, 2001; Hammond and McKinnon, 2003, Laming, 2003; Laming 2009, Department for Education, 2010). Secondly, the researcher's focus will then be on the multi-agency work and how their views are gathered about service delivery by investigating and then these views are analysed that how much effect it has and how it can be improved and also if they are producing positive results for children and their families.

Children and Young People (Scotland) Act 2014 takes GIRFEC few steps further in generating better results from infants to 18 years' professionals who comes into contact with the children must have a know how and must be comfortable with the process and procedures which also involve the use of common language and must be in accordance with the definitions of welfare and risk.

The current research will examine professional's views and experiences regarding the application of GIRFEC. It will also focus on taking into consideration of the betterment and risks, also the views of the professional must also be taken into account if it has potential of being effective in the implementation, what have been the advantages in its operation as well as the disputes and hurdles that remain between the multi-agencies.

1.2 Purpose of the Study

I am enrolled at the University of Stirling and I am a 4th year undergraduate taking course of BA (Hons) in Social Work. As an undergraduate student it is the requirement of my degree to undertake a research study to submit my dissertation. As GIRFEC is a tested and maintained national approach in order to improve the wellbeing of the children and young people residing across Scotland. The purpose of my study is to conduct a research based work which conducts a survey on professional views and experiences of applying GIRFEC. The overall ambition is to identify and analyse the strengths and weaknesses of the process since its implementation. At first, by looking at the evaluation process, methods, techniques and frameworks which are carried out to identify and guard the children and their families and also how multiple agencies working in the same environment are influenced. Its focus will then be on the multi-agency work and how their views are gathered about service delivery by investigating and then these views are analysed that how much effect it has and how it can be improved and also if they are producing positive results for children and their families.

1.3 Research Questions

1. From a professional perspective how has GIRFEC affected multi-agency working in the assessment process and service delivery for children in need of care or protection?
2. What are the perceived strengths of GIRFEC for supporting multi-agency working?
3. What are the perceived limitations?
4. Are professionals' clear of their role and duties within multi-agency working and applying GIRFEC?
5. What are the professionals' reflections on the potential impact on outcomes for children?

Chapter 2: Literature Review

Origin of GIRFEC

Getting it Right for Every Child is an approach developed by the Scottish government in order to support the wellbeing of the nation's children and young people. Support is offered and extended to them by offering them the right help at the right time (Scotland Government). The plan supports them and their parents to aid them work in partnership with the services that can assist them.

The support services that are provided for the wellbeing and rights of children and young people are prioritized for schools and for early years (Stoddart, 2015). All these services are ensured so that everyone is able to work together in order to improve outcomes for young people and for children. Many children receive support from their parents, local community and the wider family. They also receive help in partnership with services like education and health. In places and situations where extra support is needed, the GIRFEC approach aims to provide easy support in order to access child at the centre seamlessly (Parkinson, 2012).All these special services are designed for the children and young people because it is not possible for the people and communities to predict when they might need additional support.

The GIRFEC arose out of the Children's Hearing System in 2004. According to the review, in order to improve outcomes for the vulnerable children, agencies need to intervene. This intervention should be in a better and a much more integrated manner in order to identify risks and needs (Thorburn, 2014). The origin of this approach can be traced back to Kilbrandon Report published in 1964.

Implementation in the early days of this approach and its development took place in all areas and cities of Scotland. A number of projects were initiated in 2006 and were followed by an implementation phase in 2008. According to Lanarkshire report, GIRFEC led to a sharper focus on the needs of the children and it also helped to develop a culture of shared responsibility amongst different departments such as health, education and social work (Tisdall, 2015).

With a few change management elements, the implementation of GIRFEC has taken place and is in effect now. A program is designed to achieve consistency regarding the meeting of needs in order to improve outcomes for all young people and children living in Scotland

(Coles, et.al, 2016). A number of resources and guides have been published by the Scottish government in order to support the implementation of this project.

Thus, it can be said that the origin of this program is old; however, with the success of this approach, a lot of people have benefitted and even the society has grown as a whole.

Multi Agency Working

Multi agency working is an effective way of supporting children and families with additional needs in order to help to secure real improvements in the outcomes of their life. Children, in their childhood and adolescence may experience needs that might need to be highlighted (Cross, 2012). Then, there are those children who may require additional help or support as a result of a few disabilities, be it mental or physical. The living circumstances and the surrounding environment also has an impact on them, thus in order to resolve these difficulties and offer them support, a much better and effective way is multi agency working. Government strategies regarding GIRFEC report has promoted effective ways of working and has helped in improving the lives of the children as well as families (Forbes & McCartney, 2011). A duty to work together has also been a key strategy of the Scottish government regarding this approach.

Enablers and Barriers to Joint Working

Just as all other aspects of working, joint working also has a few enablers and barriers. Here are a few enablers of the approach:

Strengthening of Working Relationships

There are a number of issues related to working relationships that have been identified askey to effective joint working (Mitchell, 2011). These issues include commitment, role demarcation, respect, knowledge and trust. Working together builds an environment that helps the team to work towards the goal of the approach that has been set up, and it also helps them as to what contribution is important and how they should act. An aspect that should be considered seriously is the clarity in roles (MacQueen & McVie, 2013). If there is role ambiguity, the workers in the same team will be clueless as to what duties they have to perform.

Establishing and Reviewing Processes

Inter-agency processes are a key factor that influence the success of joint working. Consultation with service users, inclusive planning, priorities and needs are identified as integral for the implementation of joint working. Communication is key in joint working, thus maintaining a constant communication process is essential for establishing the best process in joint working (Davis, 2013). Clear strategies should be formed and all should be communicated to the workers succinctly so that there is no ambiguity as to what the whole approach is all about.

Adequate Resources

Adequate resourcing in terms of funding, staffing and time is integral and essential to the success of joint working. Financial resources are the most important resources required for this process. Adequate time allocation is another resource that is crucial for the success of this approach (Stone & Rixon, 2008). Recruitment is another resource should be sufficient in order to help the approach provide the right kind of help to children and young people when needed. Without adequate resources, the approach would be unable to offer the right kind of help to children and young people. Thus, proper financial and human resources help GIRFEC achieve its main goals and objectives.

Strong Leadership in Governance and Management

This is one of the most important characteristic of successful GIRFEC implementation. When looking to implement this approach, a strong and clear headed management is required. Lack of proper management and leadership will lead to adverse consequences (Stone & Rixon, 2008). Strong leadership provides a vision to the whole approach that is being undertaken, which is why, its absence is regarded as damaging to joint working. The management should also be able to monitor and evaluate performance in order to make sure that joint working is successful for GIRFEC.

Following are a few barriers to joint working:

Misunderstandings amongst Professionals

Professionals who are responsible to help achieve the goals of this approach need to make sure that they communicate effectively (Vincent, et.al, 2010). The essence of joint working is sharing all relevant information and communicating effectively with each other. Thus, with the risk of not sharing information appropriately amongst team members is something that should be avoided. Joint working members need to manage, analyse and evaluate a lot of aspects of information sharing as it helps in collaborating and safeguarding individuals effectively.

Cultural Barriers

Even though working with different cultures and people is encouraged everywhere, but in GIRFEC, working with different cultures impacts the safeguarding of practices undertaken by the professionals (Davis, et.al, 2012). It also affects the collaboration of agencies and impacts the working of people working together to help people achieve the goals of this objective.

Performance Assessment

It has been argued by Alexander & Sked (2010) that performance is inappropriately assessed by the management and is not scrutinised properly. This impacts how success of the program is being evaluated and judged. Individuals' performance can be assessed and scrutinised effectively; however, assessment of members in joint working is difficult and is not done effectively.

Lack of Clarity

For joint working members, it is essential that they have clarity regarding their responsibilities and are well informed of the aspects that they have to work on(Hogan, et.al, 2009). This helps them in understanding as to how they should work and what aspects they should consider when looking into aspects from different angles. However, when there are multiple agencies involved, a number of people lack clarity as to what should be done and how it should be done.

When talking about GIRFEC, none of the professionals have any ambiguity regarding their roles and responsibilities. Each one of them is clear as to what they should do and how they should act in order to help the program achieve its objective of helping children and young people whenever they need support (Tisdall, 2015).

GIRFEC Frameworks and Assessment Procedures that aid in Multi Agency Working

GIRFEC Framework focuses on these three aspects:

- The Scottish government's commitment to deliver best possible ou people, children and their families.
- The five strategic objectives of the program i.e. to make Scotland fairer and wealthier, healthier, safer and stronger, smarter and greener.
- The Care Inspectorate's Quality indicators for learning, development and training.

Scotland's policy is child centered and is influenced by the United Nations Convention on the Rights of the Child (1989). The Children's Charter (2004) was developed in consultation with children and young people as it is reflects what children and young people should expect (Scotland Government). In addition to this, a framework for standards was developed subsequently to support the charter and is a means for translating the commitments made to children. The framework identifies what each Scottish child should expect from this program, related professionals as well as agencies. This ensures them that they are protected adequately and their needs are met. The framework also includes what parents and adults should expect if they are reported for neglect and abuse.

The framework also includes the aspect that the local authorities have a duty to protect and promote the wellbeing of the children of the nation in their need area(Stradling & MacNeil, 2010). This also includes providing adequate support to families and assuring that the children are being supported and getting the best things in their life. The workforce of this program should possess the right set of skills, knowledge, understanding and should value them in order to work together to meet the needs of individuals, children and young people.

Building a competent workforce is one of the major aspects related to GIRFEC (Buchanan, 2009). Multi agency working requires all agencies to work together and build an environment where the managers of every agency works together to help support the program and contribute to help the approach achieve its goals. In addition to this, it should also be made sure that the various aspects of multi-agency working are considered to make sure that the right people are hired and that they are able to deliver as to what is required from them. A unique culture for help and support should be built wherein all people should support each other and every child should be supported (Hogan, et.al, 2009). Young people should be provided with an environment where they can discuss all their issues and look for an alternative. They can reach out to the professionals for help and support and should make sure that they receive the support they are looking for.

Policies and Assessment Tools

For assessment purposes, the National Practice Model is utilised and implemented. This model is used in a multi-agency context as well as a single agency context. This model provides a framework for the practitioners to assess the agencies and analyse their information in order to understand the needs of the children and the young people. This helps them in gathering knowledge as to who needs support and what type of help they require. It also helps in identifying the concerns that need to be addressed and promotes participation of children and young people. The national practice model includes tools like the resilience matrix, my world triangle etc. for assessment.

Risk of harm as a result of adverse factors is also assessed by the program and is one of the important factors of this approach (Holligan, et.al, 2014). Changes to legislation also helps in assessing how children and young people are impacted and how they are being looked after in this program. Injuries' compensation plans and schedules are also assessed in order to help the children and the young people who are impacted. This helps in developing policies that are effective in building a program for providing support and help to children.

Wellbeing

The overall wellbeing of a young person of a child helps in identifying any concerns related to it. The eight indicators used for wellbeing help in offering a consistent approach and language which can be used across organisational and geographical boundaries (Stoddart, 2015). These are the eight indicators that are used for defining wellbeing in the GIRFEC approach:

Safe

The safety indicator helps in identifying if the children are safe and protected from neglect, abuse and/or harm. All children and young people should also be helped to develop the right set of skills and accurate knowledge which will enable them to adopt safe practices. These practices are then implemented at school, in home or in the community where they are exposed to a higher risk of significant harm (Thorburn, 2014). On the other hand, being safe is a positive state of mind. The child or young person feels protected, safe and secured within trusted relationships. In these sort of relationships, children and young people are heard and their preferences, feelings and views are also taken into account.

Healthy

For ensuring wellbeing of the children and young people, high standards of mental and physical health are maintained. Support is also offered to them to make safe and healthy choices (Coles, et.al, 2016). If a child or a young person is physically impaired or suffers from a mental disorder, he or she possesses the right to proper and appropriate care and treatment. In addition to this, he or she is also entitled to proper and right education, training and practical support. This enables the children to manage their condition and also empowers them to develop a strong individual personality who can make decisions for themselves. Emotional health and wellbeing is also looked after under this program(Cross, 2012). Young people and children who are emotionally strong are able to manage their feelings, are motivated and are socially confident to develop the right set of skills for living independently.

Achieving

GIRFEC offers supports and guidance in learning to children and young people. They help in boosting skills, develop confidence and strong self-esteem. According to the program's Curriculum for Excellence, every child and young person has the right to fulfil his or her potential (Forbes & McCartney, 2011). Improving and enhancing attainment and achievement to improve the overall situation and to help the children and young people progress and develop the right set of skills will enable them to fulfil their potential. Curriculum for excellence explains that individual attainment is designed to raise standards and attain levels through excellence in learning and teaching. In addition to this, a child's social development is also included in achievement where their skills and confidence is developed to help them cope with different challenges of life (Thorburn, 2014).

Nurtured

All children and young people are entitled to a nurturing and stimulating place to grow and live. Nurtured is one of the childhood wellbeing domains that are usually overlooked in the quality and performance indicators. Nurturing begins in the womb when the child is impacted by the mother's actions, what she says and what she eats and drinks. The child should not be exposed to nicotine, drug or alcohol when he is in the womb (Mitchell, 2011). This impacts the health of the child, thus the nurturing aspect of wellbeing is violated. However, additional support to children and young people are offered in cases like these.

Active

Children and young people should be offered the opportunity to take part in a wide range of activities to keep them engaged. Within the GIRFEC approach, hobbies, play and recreational activities are also included in the definition of active(Davis, et.al, 2012). Development of new skills, learning how to assess and manage risks, cooperating within teams and acting responsibly are some of the major activities of wellbeing. Being active helps to develop the wellbeing of a child, develops a sense of belonging and inclusion in them, develops their emotional and physical health, enhances their sense of achievement to face new challenges and helps to develop their sense of responsibility and sense of respect(Stone & Rixon, 2008). Children and young people need a safe and secure environment to develop their personalities and need to be encouraged, thus it is essential that their activities are included and given importance.

Respected

This wellbeing indicator points out that children and young people should be involved in decision making that impact their wellbeing. They should be asked for their views and opinions on important matters that involve their safety, security and wellbeing. This will help them develop a strong personality who is capable enough to make decisions and decide what is right and what is wrong for them (Buchanan, 2009). The child's feelings of self-worth should also be considered, their self-esteem should be enhanced and the sense of being loved and cared should be taken into account when taking decisions regarding them.

Responsible

The responsibility factor does not mean that children and young people should be responsible for themselves. It is the responsibility of the program and GIRFEC is responsible for taking care of these children and young people (Davis, et.al, 2012). Not only it helps in developing them in a manner that will benefit their personality, but will also assist them in understanding as to how they should act and what aspects they should take into account. The program helps these children and young people to become responsible and be able to take decisions for themselves.

Included

This aspect helps children to overcome inequalities by proving them with the best guidance and offering help and support. In addition to this, members of the communities should also be included to help children and young people develop a sense of belonging. Inclusion is an essential aspect that should be considered in these aspects of wellbeing (Vincent, et.al, 2010). Not only it helps the children and young people in the program to develop a personality, but it also assists in developing them socially. It assists them to build and form relationships and make sure that they are a part of the society they live in.

Early Intervention, Risks and a Cultural Shift from Child Protection to Early Intervention

GIRFEC focuses on the importance of early intervention and prevention, leadership, professional workforce and high quality service provision. In order to achieve the goals of this program, it is important to create a workforce which is capable of delivering as to what the program aims to deliver. In order to assure thus, there are a few aspects that should be looked into. The first aspect relates to as to what is getting in the way of protecting a child (Forbes & McCartney, 2011). Another aspect enquires about the information that is needed to help in protecting a child. In addition to this, it should also be understood as to what should be done to protect the child, how the agency can help the child and as to what additional help may be needed or required to help protect the child.

Furthermore, the workers and managers' understanding of the concept of child protection needs to be looked into and it should be assessed as to whether they can carry out their duties effectively or not (MacQueen & McVie, 2013). Also, the related set of skills that are required for them to help them carry out their role effectively and efficiently should be looked into.

The Children and Young People Scotland Act (2014) was also established as the legislation of GIRFEC. Under this act, the Scottish government has strengthened the rights of the children and the young people. A system has been created to identify their problems at an early stage instead of waiting to act until the child or the young person reaches a critical stage.

Need for GIRFEC

GIRFEC was established for the children and young people who needed support in the community. There were instances where children and young people were left alone with no support and no help. A few of them required financial aid, some needed emotional support and some were looking to be a part of the society. Thus, all these issues caused problems and the government recognised the need for support for these type of people (Stone & Rixon, 2008). The Scottish government has now developed these set of rules under GIRFEC in order to help children and young people get the right kind of support. The program aims to help children and young people get the support and help they are looking for. In addition to this, the program also aims to treat every child equally without any discrimination.

Wellbeing Concerns

When looking into this aspect and when considering the problem of treating children and young people equally and offering them help and support, it is important for the people working for the program to understand as to how things should be shaped and how things should be managed (Buchanan, 2009). There are a number of wellbeing concerns that surround this program. GIRFEC not only assists in offering help and support to children and the young people, but it also helps in understanding as to how these people should be taken care of.

In addition to this, the wellbeing concerns also included the inclusion issues of these children and young people, their development of personalities, their individualism and how they represent themselves to the world (Alexander & Sked, 2010). This helped them in understanding as to what aspects that have to consider and what factors should be given importance to. The wellbeing concerns are taken care of in a manner by the program that adequate help and support

Chapter 3: Methodology

The third chapter of the dissertation explains the methodology endorsed in the current study. The methodology focuses on the data collected for the particular topic, the research design and it has also mentioned the sources from which data has been collected.

3.1 Research Method

The interest and idea behind the selection of the research technique is to provide new information and give an insight of the topic under discussion. The research method explains the steps taken in which the research work has been carried out. Hence, it indicates the process through which the data collection has been carried out, analysed and concluded. The results have been then presented according to Schutt (2011). Three main types of research can be carried out and they as follow:

- Constructive Research: This research method recommend solution and theories are tested according to research questions.
- Empirical Research: In this research empirical evidences are tested to provide solutions.
- Exploratory Research: This research method is carried out to identify and explain the problem.

Nonetheless, the study has adopted the exploratory research method. According to the problem statement, the method adopted to find solution for the problem is fitting as the main emphasis of the research was on explaining integration issues of Information Technology and from a professional perspective how has GIRFEC affected multi-agency working in the assessment process and service delivery for children in need of care or protection. Therefore, the exploratory research method focuses on giving the final and convincing solutions to the research questions but it also delves into the topic of research with different levels and also leave some space for the future research work in the same area (Bray, Johns and Kilburn, 2011).

3.2 Qualitative Research Method

Qualitative research techniques are most extensively used in research works by many researchers as well as quantitative and mixed research methods. The current study is based on qualitative research method as the exploratory study suggests and emphasis has been put on the identifying the problem or question. The inspiration behind the selection of qualitative research method as compare to quantitative research is to give priority to have an access to large amount of data and information. This method is basically formulated to assist the progress of researcher in getting an understanding of different perspectives of different researchers on the same topic.

Nonetheless, this research technique is cost efficient, consumes less time and does not require to conduct an extensive research. Greater number of authors either go for qualitative research or quantitative research, but most of the authors are also of the view that mixed research i.e. combination of both of the research methods, can also be adopted to find solutions. The qualitative research techniques include the sources from which data is gathered such as participant's observation, observing the environment, questionnaire, interviews, texts, documents and the author's reactions and impressions. Issue faced by many researchers who has carried out the qualitative research are suppose to publish their work in the related journals. However, most of the research works are build on the collection of large amount of data similar to the data.

3.3 Research Philosophy

This study has been developed on the positivist research philosophy. The positivist research philosophy states that reality can be described in provided and quantifiable properties that are not dependent on the researcher and his research tools. Hence, the positivist research philosophy tests the theory of the researcher and increases the scientific understanding of the overall development. Positivism comply to the fact that only knowledge provided with facts which is gained through observation (the sensibility) along with the calculations which is trustworthy. Studies carried out on the philosophy of positivism, the researcher becomes restricted to data collection and analyzing it objectively and the research findings are commonly observable and quantifiable.

Positivism is dependent on the significant observations that provides a foundation to statistical analysis. It is observed that positivism as a philosophy is in line with the empiricist view that information is originated from human experience. It has an atomistic, philosophical view of the world existing as distinct, observable aspects and occasions that communicate with a noticeable, persistent and regular manner.

Furthermore, studies with the positivism as a philosophy, the researcher is not dependent on the study and it lacks provisions for human interests. Crowther and Lancaster (2008) caution that as a common rule, positivist studies normally carries deductive research approach and inductive research access is correlated with the phenomenology philosophy. Positivism approach is related to the focal point that researcher needs to focus on the facts, on the other hand phenomenology focuses on the understanding and has provision of human interest.

3.4 Research Design

Qualitative research method has been constructed for the current study. Qualitative research design is carried out on the basis of the nature of the research and is according to the topic of the research (Schutt, 2011). The aim is to focus on the qualitative research and figure out the answer of the question or a problem without seeking or applying quantifiable measures. To accomplish the objectives of the research, qualitative research is carried out. The prime factor of qualitative research is that it suitable of small samples, whereas its results are not calculated and quantifiable. The main advantage which also comprises its basic difference with quantitative research is that it provides a thorough, complete explanation and analysis of the research topic, without any limitation to the research and the view of the author's reaction (Collis & Hussey, 2003). Nonetheless, the capability of the qualitative research is overall based on the abilities and sill of the researchers, as the results may not be considered as reliable because they most of the time comes from the author's perception and judgement and lacks objectivity. It is more suitable for small sample studies but it is also risky for the qualitative research's outcomes to be considered mirrored as the opinions of a population.

3.5 Data Collection Method

Data collection method specifies the progress of the study in which data is collected and information is computed. Methods used to collect large amount of data is categorised into two aspects, one is primary data collection process and the second is secondary data collection process. For the current research, the data has been collected by means of secondary sources as mentioned by Bray, Johns and Kilburn (2011). The secondary data collection method is based on the earlier researches related to the topic and already secondary sources for example, online databases, magazines, research articles, journals and news publications.

Prior to data collection instruments are concerned, the process of research conduction elaborated the use of semi-structured questionnaire, which served as an interview guide for the researcher. Specific questions were already assembled in way to serve as guide and accomplish the research objectives but during the interview process additional questions were also made.

3.6 Research approach

The research approach used to conduct the current research was the inductive approach. According to this approach, the research is started with the observation, which then provide the author with generalized theories and conclusions are drawn from the research. The logic behind the selection of this approach was that it takes into consideration the context where the research effort is active and also it is most suitable for small samples that provides qualitative data. On the other hand, the drawback of the inductive approach is that generalized theories are produced and the conclusions are solely based on the small samples which compromises the reliability of the research being under observation (Denzin& Lincoln, 2005).

3.7 Sample Selection

The approach of purposeful sampling was used to establish the sample for the current research. The classification of this method belongs to the non-probability sampling techniques, sample members are chosen on the grounds of their knowledge, relationship and experience and skills regarding a research subject (Freedman et al., 2007). In this research, the members chosen for this sample have a special relationship with the development under examination, adequate and related work experience in the area of social service.

Qualitative research for the current research is carried out on a small scale to conduct semi-structured interview ranging from 6-10 with professionals (social workers appointed by law, teachers and project workers on volunteer basis) working along their families who are under GIRFEC's evaluation process. Due to different funding process and smaller projects assigned to voluntary agencies, the projects assigned to the volunteers works in partnership with other experts from health who are hired by the NHS, however for the current research determination and moral approval, the researcher will conduct the interview from those who are hired by voluntary agency.

3.8 Data Analysis

Content analysis was carried out to evaluate the data which was collected by conducting personal interviews. According to Moore & McCabe (2005), the current research falls under the category which has themes and sub-themes so it can be compared. One of the major advantage of carrying content analysis is that the data collected during the interview can be reduced and made simple while at the same time the results calculated can be analysed by using quantitative techniques. In addition, content analysis guides the researcher to construct the qualitative data collected in order that satisfy and meet with the research objectives. Also, human error also has its effect in content analysis which has its own risk which is the inclusion of subjectivity and misinterpretation of the data collected during the interviews which gives rise to false and unreliable results.

Chapter 4: Ethical Consideration

In order to respect the privacy and identity of the volunteers, data will be recorded and maintained in strict confidence and the researcher has to make sure that the author will take care of the identity and views of the volunteers should be presented anonymously in the publication and volunteers should not be named and should be mentioned by 1, 2, 3, etc. Each volunteer's names should be written and recorded in an individual folders named by volunteer 1, 2, 3, etc. which provides the researcher a feasibility and can have an easy access to the data which can be maintained or destroyed if the volunteers want to withdraw their participation in the study.

When data is collected from selected volunteers, the researcher will have to be aware and responsive to their opinions, experience and beliefs as the researcher do not want to give any impression that their area of expertise, experience, knowledge and their line of work is being judged or analysed critically. Hence, the author has to specify and make sure that the reason for which the current study is conducted is clear from the very beginning along with what the author's intention is with the data collected.

The author will also have to be aware of the time, resources and location for gathering the information along with the acceptance of every volunteer to allow for privacy. Before starting the interview, researcher at first need to give an insight of the purpose and the design of the interview to the volunteers.

The researcher will administer the emotions and reactions of the volunteers with the help of support and guidelines of my supervisor during supervision in addition to keep the anonymity of the involvement in the research.

Once the study is completed, the information gathered will be erased and every volunteer will be provided with the guideline of how to gain access to finished publication of information. The research can not gain access to the personal information for example, age range or gender which is another step to guard the information of the volunteer which will take years of experience to maintain the confidentiality of the participants. The research worker will also make sure that the confidentiality of the agencies will be maintained by the protocols specified by the agencies so their ethical norms are protected.

Chapter 5: Analysis

Perceived strengths of GIRFEC for supporting multi-agency working

When respondents were asked about GIRFEC supporting the multi-agency working, then there were different views which were combined by the researcher that reveals the strength in the multi-agency working. One of the respondents' views have been provided below:

"It is good to see GIRFEC supporting multi-agency working for a good cause, the reason is because when people from different organizations attempt to aid children then it is imperative that the various needs of these children be fulfilled, and therefore the target of GIRFEC is also achieved."

While observing the response which have been made by the above respondent, the implication could be made that when multi-agency teams works in a particular project, it becomes an important consideration for the children in need. It remains a better option for these children to receive a care through a collaboration between two or more agencies. Also, another implication could be made is with regards to the targets which have been set by the Scottish government an GIRFEC regarding caring for children which is also met. Another respondent was reported saying that the following:

"I always have a perception that people in greater quantity helping someone in need would tend to create a larger difference than only one individual helping a person in need. Therefore, I believe that multi-agency working solves a problem which has long been prolonging in our society."

The implication of the above respondent could be made as there have been various issues and problems surrounding the environment, it is better that these problems are resolved by a number of organizations which have the same goals along with the same aims. When different minds tend to combine, collaborate, and communicate, then there are better chances to reach towards a constructive conclusion.

Perceived limitations of GIRFEC for supporting multi-agency working

According to the views of respondents, there could also be various limitations regarding GIRFEC supporting the multi-agency working. One of the respondents who was interviewed by the researcher made a clear point according to the following statement:

"I perceive that although multi-agency working could be overall good for the children and for the government, but a light must also be shed on the time that shall be consumed in taking a particular decision. Change in strategy from each of the organization and agreeing on a same platform may result in consuming a lot of time."

There is often the case when various individuals or organizations and agencies tend to combine together for a special cause, then there could be conflict in the partnership as each agency have different culture and a varied style of working. Along with this, there are reasons to believe that the time which is going to be consumed by these agencies in solving an issue would be higher than if the particular issue were to be resolved by a single agency. Furthermore, these agencies will have a separate vision and achieving the particular vision will require devising separate strategies in reaching to a conclusion.

Professionals' of their role and duties within multi-agency working and applying GIRFEC

According to one of the respondent, he was quoted saying the following:

"Defining the roles and responsibilities of individuals in the multi-agency working can be tough at times, not because of the single role could be offered to various individuals, but because there could be a conflict in making decisions within the organization."

According to the roles and duties of professionals, the respondents have agreed the roles and responsibilities of professionals working in the multi-agency that it may cause conflict within the two organizations. However, a sustainable business model must be comprised amongst these companies which would therefore allow the prevention of such undesirable activities. Along with this, rules and duties could be beneficial where each individual would enhance their learning from other counterparts.

Professionals' reflection on the potential impact on outcomes for children

The respondents were quoted saying the following:

"If there had not been a potential impact on the outcomes for children then the particular working would not have been granted by the GIRFEC or the Scottish government. According to my views, it has helped children in many different ways because of the fact that it has resulted in working of these agencies in remote areas where access could not have been possible."

The above statement could be understood in a way that the Scottish government and GIRFEC is doing a wonderful job in providing necessary care for children which may therefore improve their lifestyle and enhances their day-to-day activities in their life financially.

Views on GIRFEC affected by multi-agency working in the assessment process and service delivery for children in need of care or protection

"Multi-agency could be a differentiating factor in countries where there is a higher need for children care. A strong collaboration within the two or more agencies can help these children improving their lives which what matters in the end."

The majority of respondents have agreed on the statement that multi-agency working which has been supported by GIRFEC has been a differentiating factor for the purpose that it has allowed a mutual collaboration in solving the issues of the society which are related to children. These agencies have taken the matters in their hands to serve the society and respond accordingly which have therefore resulted in positive outcome.

Chapter 6: Conclusion

GIRFEC approach was carried out in this research in order to test the effectiveness, durability and strength along with its shortcomings, which works for the betterment of children and youth of Scotland (Government of Scotland, 2015). The study carried out by the author is to understand the interpretation and calculations of the multiple agencies that work for this cause.The existences of these agencies is not a new thing in Scottish environment and with the participation of parents and these agencies, the researcher found that for many years now, working of the agencies together in order to support team work had been encouraged.

As the collaboration of the parents and multiple agencies has its perks and showed better results over the years, there were many researches that showed that in some agencies, they lacked team work and they were not compatible and because of that it resulted into deaths of many children across the UK (Hammond, 2001; Hammond and McKinnon, 2003, Laming, 2003; Laming 2009, Department for Education, 2010). Researcher in the current study focal point revolved around the idea of how the agencies carried out their investigations and if it had shown any better results for the parents and their children.

In 2014 Scottish Government has passed an Act, Children and Young People (Scotland) Act, which had helped the GIRFEC approach to work better with the professionals, who had expertise in their line of work and had an in depth knowledge of their profession and they shared the use of common language to understand their patients and work efficiently for the sake of children and young people.

The study focused on the professional views and their expertise in order to understand the operations of the GIRFEC. The focus is not limited to the views and expertise but with the inclusion of the barriers and conflicts that remain among the multi-agencies.

As the area of research is quite vast and the author had narrowed down the research to series of question which were later investigated. The researcher had answered during the research that from expert's point of view how GIRFEC had affected the multiple agencies working together during their evaluation process and services were delivered to those children who were in need of care or protection. The researcher also worked on the analysis of the multiple agencies working together who supported GIRFEC and their strengths and weakness were also observed. Role and responsibilities of the experts were also analysed working under GIRFEC and what was their reaction on the results after the evaluation.

The methodology that was carried out for the current research was exploratory research which was a befitting approach as it has focused on the unification of Information Technology and from a professional perspective how has GIRFEC affected multi-agency working in the assessment process and service delivery for children in need of care or protection(Bray, Johns and Kilburn, 2011). The qualitative approach was used instead of quantitative approach because it enabled the researcher to have an access to the pool of data and information and also this method has proved to be a better option to find out answers for the research questions because of the small sample research (Collis & Hussey, 2003). Along with these methods, source used for data collection process was the secondary data collection process. The sample selected for the study ranged from 6-10 members and with professionals (social workers appointed by law, teachers and project workers on volunteer basis) working along their families who were under GIRFEC's evaluation process. These volunteers were evaluated on the basis of semi-structured interview. Further, for the evaluation of the data gathered content analysis technique was used which also ensured the safety, confidentiality and privacy of the information that was gathered during the data collection process. Despite a role that can be played by subjectivity, content analysis is a good technique to satisfy and meet the research objectives.

The results revealed that the majority of respondents had a support for GIRFEC which had been supporting the multi-agency teams for the purpose of looking after the children in need. The strengths of the multi-agency working included a better collaboration, mutual working, awareness of the project, better care for children, and a better solution for a problem when a combination of different social workers and volunteers are present to care for the children. However, at the same time the volunteers and the social workers also believe that there are certain limitations which also need lights to be shed. The respondents believe that when there are various individuals involved in solving a particular problem or to provide care for children, then it is often time consuming because it takes longer than normal in reaching a conclusion. Furthermore, other limitation may also include chances of conflicts, development of a longer chain where there could be lack of communication. However, the researcher has reached to a conclusion that there has been a positive impact of GIRFEC supporting the multi-agency working which aids in a quick and steadfast delivery of service for children. Therefore, it is recommended to the Scottish authorities and government to focus on decreasing the limitations which have emerged during the working of multi-agency teams.

Chapter 7: Evaluation

The researcher wanted to identify if there is a potential impact of GIRFEC supporting the multi-agency working and if it helps in better service process and service delivery for the care of children. The results identified from 8 respondents who were the social workers and volunteers in an agency, it revealed that GIRFEC supporting the multi-agency working has a strong potential impact. It was further revealed that there were strengths of the agencies working together while at the same time limitations for the agencies working together. However, the majority percentage of respondents claimed that there had been a supporter of the multi-agency working for the benefit of the children. It has also provided variety of solutions for children in their better care in collaborating with their parents. The particular has allowed the researcher in gaining an insight on the working of the social workers.

References

Alexander, S. & Sked, H., 2010. The development of solution focused multi- agency meetings in a psychological service. Educational Psychology in Practice, 26(3), pp.239-249

Bray, J., Johns, N. and Kilburn, D., 2011. An exploratory study into the factors impeding ethical consumption. Journal of business ethics, 98(4), pp.597-608.

Buchanan, G., 2009. Child protection and risk–the relationship between risk assessment and getting it right for every child (GIRFEC). Review of national child protection guidance. Scottish Government, Edinburgh

Coles, E., Cheyne, H., Rankin, J. and Daniel, B., 2016. Getting It Right for Every Child: A National Policy Framework to Promote Children's Well- being in Scotland, United Kingdom. The Milbank Quarterly, 94(2), pp.334-365

Collis, J.H. and Hussey, R., R.(2003). Business Research-A practical guide for undergraduate and postgraduate students. Hampshire: Palgrave Macmillan.

Coulshed, V. & Orme, J (2006) *Social Work Practice,* Basingstoke, Palgrave Macmillan.

Cross, B., 2012. Negotiating the Multiple Meanings of Participation within Multi-agency Working: children's participation at policies' crossroads. Power and Education, 4(1), pp.96-105

Crowther, D. and Lancaster, G., 2012. Research methods. Routledge.

Data retrieved from: http://www.gov.scot/Topics/People/Young-People/gettingitright, on 8th December, 2016

Davis, J.E., Davis, J.M. & Smith, M., 2012. Working in Multi-professional Contexts: A Practical Guide for Professionals in Children's Services. Sage

Davis, J.M., 2013. Supporting creativity, inclusion and collaborative multi-professional learning. Improving schools, 16(1), pp.5-20

Department for Education. (2006) *Working together to safeguard children: A guide to inter-agency working to safeguard and promote the welfare of children*, The Stationery Office [Online] Available at: https://www.gov.uk/government/uploads/system/uploads/attachment_data/file/419595/W orking_Together_to_Safeguard_Children.pdf

Department for Eduction. (2010) *Haringey Local Safeguarding Children Board Serious Case Review 'Child A',* Department for Education.

Education Scotland. (2012) *Getting it right for every child: Where are we now?,* Livingston, Education Scotland.

Forbes, J. & McCartney, E., 2011. Educating Scotland's future together?: Inter/professional preparation for schools and children's services. Scottish Educational Review, pp.39-54

Hammond, E., McKinnon, E. and Nolan, D., 2010. Human Immunodeficiency Virus Treatment—Induced Adipose Tissue Pathology and Lipoatrophy: Prevalence and Metabolic Consequences. Clinical Infectious Diseases, 51(5), pp.591-599.

HMSO   (1995)   *The   Kilbrandon   Report,*   Edinburgh   [Online]   Available   at: http://www.gov.scot/Resource/Doc/47049/0023863.pdf(Accessed 07/06/2015).

Hogan, S., Dogra, N. & Kitchen, C., 2009. Multi-agency working. Nursing in Child and Adolescent Mental Health, pp.134-144

Holligan, C., Hanson, L., Henderson, G. & Adams, M., 2014. The 'Care'of Children in Need in Contemporary Scotland The Role of Positivism and Performance Indicators in Official Imaginings of Childhood and Wellbeing. Scottish Journal of Residential Child Care, 13(1)

Laming, L. (2003) *Inquiry into the death of Victoria Climbié, London,* Stationery Office.

Leathard, A. (2003) *Interprofessional collaboration: From policy to practice in health and social care,* Hove, Brunner and Routledge

Lord, L. (2009) *The Protection of Children in England: A progress report, London,* The Stationery Office.

MacQueen, S. & McVie, S., 2013. The Whole System Approach for Children and Young People who Offend: An Evaluation of Early Stage Implementation. Glasgow, University of Edinburgh. SCCJR Briefing Paper, 1, p.201.

Maxwell, J, A. (2013) *Qualitative research design: An interactive approach,* 3rd edn, London, Sage Publications Inc.

Mitchell, F., 2011. Enablers and barriers to joint working. A Briefing. Scottish Child Care and Protection Network

Moore, D.S., McCabe, G.P. and Evans, M.J., 2005. Introduction to the practice of statistics Minitab manual and Minitab version 14. WH Freeman &Co..

Norman K. Denzin and Yvonna S. Lincoln, 2005. The Sage handbook of qualitative research. Sage.

O'Brien, S., McKinnon, M. and Hammond, H. (2003) *Report of the Caleb Ness inquiry*, City of Edinburgh Council.

Parkinson, J., 2012. Establishing a core set of national, sustainable mental health indicators for children and young people in Scotland: Final Report. NHS Health Scotland

Robson, C. (2002) *General design issues in real world research: A resource for social scientists and practioner-researcher*, 2nd edn, Oxford, Blackwell

Schutt, R.K., 2011. Investigating the social world: The process and practice of research. Pine Forge Press.

Scottish Children's Reporter Administration (2014) *The Children's Panel: Some key statistics* [Online] Available at: https://www.childrenspanelscotland.org/some-key-statistics/(Accessed 07/06/2015).

Scottish Executive (2001) *For Scotland's children: Better integrated children's services,*Edinburgh, The Stationery Office [Online] Available at: http://www.gov.scot/Resource/Doc/1141/0105219.pdf (Accessed 07/06/2015)

Scottish Government (1968) *Social work (Scotland) Act 1968* [Online] Available at: http://www.legislation.gov.uk/ukpga/1968/49/contents (Accessed 07/06/2015).

Scottish Government (2011) *The Children's Hearing (Scotland) Act 2011* [Online] Available at: http://www.legislation.gov.uk/asp/2011/1/contents(Accessed 07/06/2015).

Scottish Government. (2006)*Getting it Right for Every Child Consultation Pack on the Review of the Children's Hearings System* [Online] Available at: http://www.gov.scot/Publications/2004/04/19283/36192. (Accessed 07/06/2015).

Scottish Government. (2014a) *Children and Young People (Scotland) Act 2014* [Online] Available at: http://www.legislation.gov.uk/asp/2014/8/contents/enacted(Accessed 07/06/2015).

Scottish Government. (2014b) *National guidance for child protection in Scotland 2014,* [Online] Available at: http://www.cne-siar.gov.uk/childProtectionCommittee/documents/Guidelines2014.pdf, (Accessed 07/06/2015).

Scottish Government. (2015) *Children's Hearings* [Online] Available at: http://www.gov.scot/Topics/People/Young-People/protecting/childrens-hearings. (Accessed 07/06/2015).

Scottish Government. (2015)*Children and Young People (Scotland) Act 2014: The Scottish Government response to the consultation on the draft statutory guidance parts 4, 5 & 18 (Section 96)*, Scottish Government, Edinburgh.

Stoddart, E., 2015. The Named Person: Surveillance and the wellbeing of children and young people in Scotland. Surveillance & Society, 13(1), p.102

Stone, B. & Rixon, A., 2008. Towards integrated working. Changing Children's Services: Working and Learning Together, pp.49-92

Stradling, B. & MacNeil, M., 2010. Getting it right for every child (GIRFEC) Evaluation themed briefing: Briefing 5 outcomes for children and young people. Edinburgh, Scottish Government

Thorburn, M., 2014. Educating for well-being in Scotland: policy and philosophy, pitfalls and possibilities. Oxford Review of Education, 40(2), pp.206-222

Tisdall, E.K.M., 2015. Children's Rights and Children's Wellbeing: Equivalent Policy Concepts?. Journal of Social Policy, 44(4), pp.807-823

Vincent, S., Daniel, B. & Jackson, S., 2010. Where now for 'child protection'in Scotland?. Child Abuse Review, 19(6), pp.438-456

Whittaker, A. (2012) *Research skills for social work*, London, Sage Publications.

Appendix I- Interview Questions

Q1: Can you provide some of the perceived strengths of GIRFEC for supporting multi-agency working?

Q2: What could be the perceived limitations of GIRFEC for supporting multi-agency working?

Q3: Do you think professionals are clear of their role and duties within multi-agency working and applying GIRFEC

Q4: What are your professionals' reflections on the potential impact on outcomes for children?

Q5: According to your views, how has GIRFEC affected multi-agency working in the assessment process and service delivery for children in need of care or protection?

YOUR KNOWLEDGE HAS VALUE

- We will publish your bachelor's and
  master's thesis, essays and papers

- Your own eBook and book -
  sold worldwide in all relevant shops

- Earn money with each sale

Upload your text at www.GRIN.com
and publish for free